building up
your
spouse

homebuilders
COUPLES SERIES®

building up your spouse

by
dennis & barbara
rainey

FamilyLife Publishing®
Little Rock, Arkansas

BUILDING UP YOUR SPOUSE
FamilyLife Publishing®
5800 Ranch Drive
Little Rock, Arkansas 72223
1-800-FL-TODAY • FamilyLife.com

FLTI, d/b/a FamilyLife®, is a ministry of Campus Crusade for Christ International®

Previously published under the title *Building Your Mate's Self-Esteem*

Scripture quotations are from The Holy Bible, English Standard Version, copyright © 2001 by Crossway Bibles, a division of Good News Publishers. Used by permission. All rights reserved.

ISBN: 978-1-60200-329-3

Design: Brand Navigation, LLC

Cover image: © Jupiter Images/Tammy Hanratty

Printed in the United States of America

17 16 15 14 13   7 8 9 10 11

Unless the Lord builds the house,
those who build it labor in vain.

PSALM 127:1

The HomeBuilders Couples Series®

Building Your Marriage to Last
Improving Communication in Your Marriage
Resolving Conflict in Your Marriage
Mastering Money in Your Marriage
Building Teamwork in Your Marriage
Growing Together in Christ
Building Up Your Spouse
Managing Pressure in Your Marriage

The HomeBuilders Parenting Series®

Improving Your Parenting
Establishing Effective Discipline for Your Children
Guiding Your Teenagers
Raising Children of Faith

Marriage should be enjoyed, not endured. It is meant to be a vibrant relationship between two people who love each other with passion, commitment, understanding, and grace. So secure is the bond God desires between a husband and a wife that He uses it to illustrate the magnitude of Christ's love for the church (Ephesians 5:25-33).

Do you have that kind of love in your marriage?

Relationships often fade over time as people drift apart—but only if the relationship is left unattended. We have a choice in the matter; our marriages don't have to grow dull. Perhaps we just need to give them some attention.

That's the purpose behind the HomeBuilders Couples Series®— to provide you a way to give your marriage the attention it needs and deserves. This is a biblically based small-group study because, in the Bible, God has given the blueprint for building a loving and secure marriage. His plan is designed to enable a man and a woman to grow together in a mutually satisfying relationship and then to reach out to others with the love of Christ. Ignoring God's plan may lead to isolation and, in far too many cases, the breakup of the home.

Whether your marriage needs a complete makeover or just a few small adjustments, we encourage you to consult God's design. Although written nearly two thousand years ago, Scripture still speaks clearly and powerfully about the conflicts and challenges men and women face.

Do we really need to be part of a group? Couldn't we just go through this study as a couple?

While you could work through the study as a couple, you would miss the opportunity to connect with friends and to learn from one another's experiences. You will find that the questions in each session not only help you grow closer to your spouse, but they also create an environment of warmth and fellowship with other couples as you study together.

What does it take to lead a HomeBuilders group?

Leading a group is much easier than you may think, because the leader is simply a facilitator who guides the participants through the discussion questions. You are not teaching the material but are helping the couples discover and apply biblical truths. The special dynamic of a HomeBuilders group is that couples teach themselves.

The study guide you're holding has all the information and guidance you need to participate in or lead a HomeBuilders group. You'll find leader's notes in the back of the guide, and additional helps are posted online at FamilyLife.com/Resources.

What is the typical schedule?

Most studies in the HomeBuilders Couples Series are six to eight weeks long, indicated by the number of sessions in the guide. The sessions are designed to take sixty minutes in the group with a project for the couples to complete between sessions.

Isn't it risky to talk about your marriage in a group?

The group setting should be enjoyable and informative—and non-threatening. THREE SIMPLE GROUND RULES will help ensure that everyone feels comfortable and gets the most out of the experience:

1. Share nothing that will embarrass your spouse.
2. You may pass on any question you do not want to answer.
3. If possible, as a couple complete the HomeBuilders project between group sessions.

What other help does FamilyLife offer?

Our list of marriage and family resources continues to grow. Visit FamilyLife.com to learn more about our:

- Weekend to Remember® marriage getaway, The Art of Marriage®, Stepping Up™, and other events;
- slate of radio broadcasts, including the nationally syndicated *FamilyLife Today*®, *Real FamilyLife*® *with Dennis Rainey*, and *FamilyLife This Week*®;
- multimedia resources for small groups, churches, and community networking;
- interactive products for parents, couples, small-group leaders, and one-to-one mentors; and
- assortment of blogs, forums, and other online connections.

Dennis Rainey is the president and CEO of FamilyLife (a ministry of Campus Crusade for Christ) and a graduate of Dallas Theological Seminary. For more than thirty-five years, he has been speaking and writing on marriage and family issues. Since 1976, he has overseen the development of FamilyLife's numerous outreaches, including the popular Weekend to Remember marriage getaway. He is also the daily host of the nationally syndicated radio program *FamilyLife Today*®. Barbara is an artist and author. Her books include *Thanksgiving: A Time to Remember, Barbara and Susan's Guide to the Empty Nest,* and *When Christmas Came.* The Raineys have six children and numerous grandchildren.

contents

There's an old song made popular by Kenny Rogers: "She Believes in Me." The lyrics celebrate the courage that love can bring. It's a recognition of the truth that is known in the heart of every husband and wife—that as long as our spouse believes in us, we don't care how many are against us. The love and loyalty of one counts for more than the accusations and insults of the many.

Amazing, isn't it, just how much difference a spouse can make in our level of confidence and courage? For the good or the bad.

To be clear, we're not talking about conceit; we're talking about confidence. The kind of confidence that comes from a clear understanding of who and what we are as children of God. Confidence to accept each other and to help each other be all that God wants us to be as individuals, as spouses, and as families.

May you find in these pages, and in your interaction with your group, a new level of confidence that will strengthen your marriage and make God's work evident to all.

—Dennis & Barbara Rainey

1 Giving Strength to the
One You Love

Marriage provides one of life's best relationships for building a person's confidence and courage.

The Day We Wed

Have each couple introduce themselves by answering one of the following questions about the day they were married:

- What was the weather like?
- Who traveled the farthest to attend your wedding?
- What special song was sung?
- What happened that you didn't expect?

blueprints

The Need

1. One of the greatest needs of every individual is to be built up—to be encouraged or strengthened—in the task of living. What are some reasons for this?

2. How we think about ourselves plays a huge role in how we live our daily lives. How does your self-perception affect you?

   - Positively

   - Negatively

3. Scripture often exhorts Christians to build up one another. How do you think 1 Thessalonians 5:11 applies to a married couple? What are some ways you can build up each other in your marriage relationship?

4. Read the following passages, and discuss how they relate to building up one's spouse.

   • Romans 15:5–7

   • Ephesians 4:29–32

Let's look at some of the forces that shape the way we think about ourselves.

A Phantom Standard

You have a mental image of how you should act as a husband or wife, and chances are this image is so idealistic that it is completely unattainable. Yet every day you judge your performance by this phantom! And since you cannot match those standards, your confidence suffers. Read the descriptions of "The Perfect Wife" and "The Perfect Husband," then answer the questions that follow.

The Perfect Wife

She is always loving, patient, and understanding. She is well organized, with a perfect balance of being disciplined and flexible. Her house is always neat and well-decorated, and her children obey her every command. She never gets angry with her children, even when they forget to do their chores. She is energetic and never tired, even after working all day and getting up five times during the night to tend her children. She reaches out to her neighbors and takes meals to the sick and needy. She looks fresh and attractive at all times, whether relaxing in jeans and a sweater, digging in the garden, or going out to dinner in a silk dress. Her hair always does what she wants it to do. Her fingernails are never broken. She always plans healthy, balanced meals for her family and bakes everything from scratch. She walks faithfully with God every day and studies and memorizes scripture.

The Perfect Husband

He rises early, has a quiet time reading the Bible and praying, and then jogs several seven-minute miles. After breakfast with his family, he presents a fifteen-minute devotional. He never forgets to hug and kiss his wife good-bye. He arrives at work ten minutes early. He is consistently patient with his coworkers, always content with his job, and devises creative solutions to problems. He works hard and never wastes time. His desk is never cluttered, and he is confidently in control at all times. He is well-read in world events, politics, and important social issues. He is a handyman around the house and loves to build things for his family. He arrives home from work on time every day and never turns down a request to play with his children. He is popular with everyone he meets and never tires of helping people in need. He can quote large sections of Scripture in a single bound, has faith more powerful than a locomotive, and is faster than a speeding bullet when solving family conflicts. He never gets discouraged, never wants to quit, and always has the right words for any circumstance. He never loses things, always flosses his teeth, has no trouble with his weight, and has time to fish.

5. Take two or three minutes to write a description of your phantom.

6. What impact does the phantom have on your confidence as a spouse? As a parent?

A New Standard

7. Some followers of Christ raise an important issue of whether it is biblical to talk about building our confidence or, as some have called it, our self-esteem. Indeed, Romans 12:3 says, "I say to everyone among you not to think of himself more highly than he ought to think." It is true that we are flawed human beings who need God's grace and forgiveness, but the Bible provides additional insights about how God views us. What do the following passages say about the value God places on each person?

- Genesis 1:26–28, 31

- Psalm 139:13–16

- Matthew 10:29–31

- John 3:16–17

- Ephesians 2:10

8. Why are these truths difficult to grasp on a daily basis?

9. A. W. Tozer once wrote, "What comes into our minds when we think about God is the most important thing about us." Why is it important to think rightly about God? How might our view of God affect how we think of ourselves?

10. How can you help your spouse think rightly about God?

homebuilders principle: As you and your spouse understand who God is and the value you have to Him, you can help each other slay your phantoms and start the process of becoming all God wants you to be.

make a date

Set a time for you and your spouse to complete the HomeBuilders project together before the next group meeting. You will be asked at the next session to share an insight or experience from the project.

date _____ time _____

location _____

homebuilders project

On Your Own

Answer the following questions:

1. Self-Esteem Inventory

> **Read through the following list of descriptions, then use the letters shown to rank how each description fits you.**
>
> **U = Usually   S = Sometimes   R = Rarely**
>
> ___ fearful of change
>
> ___ fearful of rejection
>
> ___ identify with accomplishments
>
> ___ critical of self
>
> ___ easily discouraged
>
> ___ preoccupied with the past
>
> ___ defensive
>
> ___ driven by performance
>
> ___ seek identity through position
>
> ___ indecisive
>
> ___ critical of others
>
> ___ compare myself with others
>
> ___ fearful of failure
>
> ___ tend to believe the worst about a situation
>
> ___ can be paralyzed by my inadequacies
>
> ___ seek identity through accumulation of wealth
>
> ___ have difficulty establishing meaningful relationships
>
> ___ hide weaknesses
>
> ___ attempt to control others to make myself look good
>
> ___ seek identity through association with significant others
>
> ___ overly self-conscious
>
> ___ have unreal expectations of myself
>
> ___ need continual approval
>
> ___ have difficulty opening up

2. Go back through the descriptions and put a star next to the two or three that you struggle with most.

3. Look at the list once more and mark the two or three areas you think your spouse struggles with most.

With Your Spouse

1. Share with each other the results of the Self-Esteem Inventory.

2. How well did you assess where your spouse struggles the most with self-esteem? What ranking, if any, surprised you?

3. Discuss one or two ways you could better support each other in the areas where you struggle.

4. Together read 2 Corinthians 12:9–10. Discuss what this passage reveals about how Paul viewed his weaknesses and what application you could make of his view.

5. Read the following personal pledge statement with your spouse:

I pledge to you that I will use the next six sessions of this HomeBuilders study to build, strengthen, and encourage our marriage. I will make this study a priority in my schedule by faithfully keeping our dates, working through the projects, and participating in the group discussions.

Will you honor your spouse by making this pledge to him or her? If so, sign the pledge in your spouse's book.

(your spouse's signature) _____

6. Close by praying for each other. Thank God for your spouse. Ask God to use you to help your spouse see who he or she is in His eyes. And ask God to use your weaknesses as an opportunity to demonstrate His power in your lives.

Remember to take your calendar to the next session for Make a Date.

2

Unconditional
Acceptance

Spouses can give each other the liberating power
of unconditional love.

Best Friends

Share with the group your answer to one of the following questions:

- Who was your best friend when you were growing up, and
  what made you close?
- Think about someone who helped you make the transition
  to a new school, job, neighborhood, or church. What did
  that person do that helped you most?
- What's the closest group or team that you've been a
  part of?

Project Report

If you completed the HomeBuilders project from the first session, share one thing you learned.

blueprints

One of the greatest human needs is to be unconditionally loved and accepted. Unfortunately, the fear of rejection is a controlling influence in many lives and marriages.

A Controlling Influence

1. Read Genesis 3:1–10. In this passage Adam and Eve hid from God. What did they fear? How common do you think this fear is today?

2. Why do people fear rejection?

3. What are some ways that the fear of rejection can affect a marriage relationship?

4. Read Ephesians 2:4–7. What do you find in these verses about your ultimate acceptance by God?

homebuilders principle: To experience a healthy marriage, you must strive to unconditionally love and accept your spouse.

Commitment to Acceptance

5. Read Genesis 2:21–24. What components of acceptance do you see in these verses? How do these verses demonstrate Adam's commitment to acceptance?

6. While it may be true that opposites attract, it is also true that the differences that first attracted you to your spouse can later become sources of aggravation.

   • What are some ways, other than physically, that you and your spouse are different?

   • How have you seen God use these differences in your marriage?

7. What is one way you can demonstrate your commitment to accepting your spouse?

Demonstration of Love

As you have probably already discovered, words or acts that communicate love and acceptance to you don't always communicate the same message to your spouse. You may have to change the way you convey your message so that he or she can feel loved and accepted.

8. Review the following elements of love taken from 1 Corinthians 13:4–8, and answer the questions that follow. (Answer these questions individually first, then share your responses with your spouse.)

Love . . .

is patient	keeps no record of wrongs
is kind	does not delight in evil
does not envy	rejoices with the truth
does not boast	always protects
is not proud	always trusts
is not rude	always hopes
is not self-seeking	always perseveres
is not easily angered	never fails

- Which elements of love in this list is your spouse particularly good at demonstrating? Specifically, what does he or she say or do that makes you feel this way?

- What element of love do you desire to do a better job of expressing toward your spouse? What is one way you could begin to do that?

9. Read 1 John 4:18. How does this verse describe the effect of love?

homebuilders principle: Only as your spouse experiences the security of your unconditional love will he or she risk being vulnerable in your marriage relationship.

make a date

Set a time for you and your spouse to complete the HomeBuilders project together before the next group meeting. You will be asked at the next session to share an insight or experience from the project.

date _____ time _____

location _____

homebuilders project

On Your Own

Answer the following seven questions:

1. What is one of the most meaningful expressions of love that your spouse has shown you?

2. What is one way your spouse expresses love and acceptance to you that you appreciate?

3. In what areas of your life are you feeling confident and accepted right now?

4. In what areas are you fearful or afraid of rejection? What effect is this having on you?

5. In what way, if any, are you making it difficult for your spouse to be more transparent with you?

6. How can you better express to your spouse the kind of love that "casts out fear" (1 John 4:18)?

7. How would you like for your spouse to pray for you? List at least three ways.

With Your Spouse

1. Share your answers to the seven questions above.

2. Share one insight you have gained about your spouse from this session.

3. Together read Romans 15:7. How are you doing at accepting each other?

4. Finish by praying for each other in the areas you noted above. Thank God for your spouse.

Remember to take your calendar to the next session for Make a Date.

For Extra Impact

Love note: As a couple, you may want to consider doing this exercise to further communicate and reinforce your commitment to accepting each other.

On a separate piece of paper, write out a one- or two-paragraph statement expressing love, commitment, and acceptance for your spouse. Be sure to include a statement about casting out fear of rejection. Sign, date, and deliver your note.

3

Putting the Past
in Perspective

Understanding how the past has affected a spouse's
self-perception can build hope and perspective.

Down Memory Lane

1. Share a childhood memory recalled by one of these
   questions:

   - What positive experience—a particular accomplishment,
     for example, or a comment someone made about you—
     still makes you feel good?
   - What not-so-positive experience—perhaps an embarrass-
     ing moment—can you laugh about today although the
     memory still makes you cringe?

2. In general, when you think back to your childhood, how do you feel?

- I get butterflies in my stomach, and my palms get sweaty.
- I'm glad it's over.
- I wish I could do it all over again.
- It makes me smile.
- Other: _____.

Project Report

Share one thing you learned from the HomeBuilders project from last session.

A Special Message

Even when we don't realize it, past mistakes and wrong choices, including those made by others, can have a profound impact on us today. This session may touch on some sensitive areas from the past. Our intent is not to embarrass anyone or to reopen old wounds or to create guilt for something God has already forgiven. Rather, our hope is that two things will occur:

- You will recognize the impact the past has had on you for good and bad.

- You will learn biblical principles that will help put the past behind you.

You and your spouse can build a relationship in which you lovingly remind each other of God's forgiveness. However, if there is something you cannot work through, we recommend you ask for help from your pastor or a competent Christian counselor.

Throughout this session and the HomeBuilders project, remember not to share anything that would embarrass your spouse or that might not be safe.

The Effect of the Past

1. One area of the past that will always affect you is your relationship with your parents. How have these relationships affected your life . . .

   - Positively

   - Negatively

2. What other individuals—friends, siblings, teachers, etc.—had a significant influence on who you are today?

3. We can see an example of how the past affects us when we
   look at an episode in the life of King David.

   • Read 2 Samuel 11. What sins did David commit?

   • Read Psalm 51. What sense do you get about how David
     is feeling? What insights about dealing with the past do
     you gain from his example?

homebuilders principle: To put the past behind you and
have hope for the future, you and your spouse must experience
and express God's forgiveness through Jesus Christ.

Encouragement from the Word

4. Read Isaiah 43:18–19. What encouragement do these verses
   give you for the future?

5. Before becoming a follower of Christ, Paul actively perse-
cuted Christians (see Acts 8:3; 22:4). Through Christ he was
able to put his past behind him. Let's look at scriptures from
the writings of Paul that can help us deal with our pasts.
What hope or encouragement for the future do you find in
the following passages?

- Romans 8:1–2

- Romans 8:37–39

- 2 Corinthians 5:17

- Ephesians 4:32

- Philippians 3:12–14

- Philippians 4:6–7

6. Of the verses and insights that were just shared, which is most meaningful to you right now? Why?

Helping Your Spouse Put the Past in Perspective

7. We read in Ephesians 4:32 that we are to forgive "as God in Christ forgave you." How can you apply that in your marriage relationship?

8. How can you help your spouse in "forgetting what lies behind" and experiencing the reality of Philippians 3:13?

homebuilders principle: When dealing with the past, you can best help your spouse by providing love, acceptance, and forgiveness.

Accentuate the Positive

While the past provides both positive and negative influences, it's the negative ones that cause us problems in the present. As you and your spouse talk about each other's past and attempt to help each other deal with the negative situations, do not overlook the positive influences.

9. From the following list of positive attributes, select one that you feel your spouse exemplifies particularly well. Think of an occasion in your relationship when he or she demonstrated this attribute, and share it with the group.

- kindness
- generosity
- courage
- forgiveness
- patience
- discernment
- humility

make a date

Set a time for you and your spouse to complete the HomeBuilders project together before the next group meeting. You will be asked at the next session to share an insight or experience from the project.

date _____ time _____

location _____

homebuilders project

As we learned in the group session, the events of the past have a huge influence on how we view ourselves today. As you complete the following project, you will talk about different areas of the past, and you will have the opportunity to get to know each other in a deeper way.

Approach this project with caution. As you discuss both positive and negative influences from the past, remember that perhaps no area of our lives haunts us more than the mistakes we or others have made. Marriages reach different levels of maturing love, acceptance, and trust. The best advice for a project like this is to share what needs to be discussed and to put your spouse's past behind you. Never pry, and avoid unpleasant details except when it is absolutely necessary to deal with them. If sensitive areas are exposed when discussing the past, never use them to punish your spouse further. Remember, "perfect love casts out fear" (1 John 4:18).

Note: If you are in doubt about sharing something with your spouse, don't do it now. It may be necessary to seek outside counseling if substantial issues arise that cannot be, or should not be, dealt with in this context.

On Your Own

Choose one of three areas: parents, peers, or the past in general. Go to that section of this project, and answer the questions. (You and your spouse may choose different areas.)

Parents

1. Describe your home and family as you were growing up. What words come to mind?

2. What things did your mom and dad do best as parents?

   • Mom

   • Dad

3. What did they not do well?

   • Mom

   • Dad

4. Describe your relationship with each of your parents. For each parent, answer these questions:

What is your fondest memory?

- Mom

- Dad

What is one thing about your relationship you wish you could change?

- Mom

- Dad

What is the biggest impact each parent has had on you?

- Mom

- Dad

5. Describe the emotions you are feeling toward each parent right now.

- Mom

- Dad

6. If you are holding something against either or both of your parents, write a statement of how you feel, and then confess to God any bitterness, unresolved anger, or resentment as sin.

Answer question 7
if either or both of
your parents are
still living.

7. What one action do you need to take toward your parent(s)?

Peers

1. Describe the influence your peers had on you as you grew up, either for good or bad.

2. As you were growing up, what value system was held by most of your peers?

3. What influence did your peers have on who you are today? In what specific ways?

4. As you look at your past relationships with peers, are there any incidents you need to put behind you or people you need to forgive so that you can put the past in perspective (see Philippians 3:13–14)?

5. How do your current peers challenge your values and convictions, either positively or negatively?

6. Are there any relationships with peers in which you are conforming to wrong values and thus not fulfilling God's standard for you (see Romans 12:1–2)? If so, which ones, and what do you need to do about them?

The Past in General

1. Identify one person or one significant experience in the past that has greatly affected your self-esteem (for good or for bad).

2. What incidents or areas from the past continue to affect you today?

3. What is one thing from this session that you can use to deal with the past?

4. What are some practical ways your spouse can help you move beyond the past?

5. Review the Scripture passages from Blueprints questions 4 and 5 of this session. What truth in these verses speaks to you? How can you apply this to your life?

6. What are some ways you and your spouse can help each other when issues from the past come up in your marriage?

With Your Spouse

1. Share the answers you wrote from the time you spent on your own. Seek to understand where your spouse is coming from. Be an active listener, and don't condemn.

2. Share with your spouse how you felt as you worked through the questions about the past.

3. What is something your spouse can do to help you follow through with any decisions or commitments you made during this project?

4. Pray together. Look up 1 John 1:9; 2 Corinthians 5:17; and 2 Corinthians 5:21. Pray these verses back to God. Claim them as true in your life, and by faith thank God for your past.

Remember to take your calendar to the next session for Make a Date.

4

Planting
Positive Words

The words people speak have the potential to build up or tear down their spouses.

Guess Who

On a piece of paper or an index card, list three or four descriptive words or phrases about yourself, then give your list to the leader. Once all the lists are turned in, the leader will, in random order, read the lists to the group. After each description is read, write a guess as to whom it is describing. After all the lists have been read, share your guesses, and then answer the following question:

- In what way do words have the power to paint pictures in our mind?

Project Report

Share one thing you learned from the HomeBuilders project from last session.

The Power of Words

1. "Sticks and stones may break my bones, but words will never hurt me." As you look at this childhood statement from an adult perspective, how do you feel about it?

2. Think about the power of words in your life. What were some statements you heard about yourself while growing up— either positive or negative—that you still remember?

3. What is easier for you to recall—positive or negative words? Why?

4. Words can be compared to seeds. Read aloud the following verses from Proverbs about the power of words.

- Proverbs 11:9
- Proverbs 12:25
- Proverbs 15:4
- Proverbs 16:24
- Proverbs 24:26
- Proverbs 25:11

Of these verses, which truth most stands out to you and why?

The Power of Praise

Since words should be used carefully and constructively, let's consider how best to speak to your spouse.

5. What is one of the best compliments or words of encouragement you have received?

6. Why do you think some people find it hard to give or to receive praise? Which is harder for you to do?

7. Read Ruth 2:2–17. The pleasant exchange of words between Boaz and Ruth occurred in ordinary, daily circumstances as they both went about their work. In what way does their interaction challenge you in how you relate to your spouse, particularly in the words you use daily?

8. It is important to be specific in praising your spouse. Complete the following statements about your spouse:

- Thank you for . . .

- You made me feel loved when . . .

- I like being with you because . . .

- I appreciate you because . . .

- I admire you for . . .

- I feel confident that you can . . .

- One thing you are really good at is . . .

homebuilders principle: Generous praise can transform your spouse and improve your marriage.

make a date

Set a time for you and your spouse to complete the HomeBuilders project together before the next group meeting. You will be asked at the next session to share an insight or experience from the project.

date _____ time _____

location _____

homebuilders project

On Your Own

Answer the following questions:

1. During the group session, what insight, discovery, or reminder did you find most helpful?

2. Why do you think there is a tendency for couples to become callous or insensitive to the effect their words have on each other after they have been married awhile? How can understanding the power of words begin to change the vocabulary you use with your spouse?

3. What are some words from your spouse that encourage you and lift your spirit?

4. What are some words from your spouse that bring you down and discourage you?

5. How can you more regularly communicate praise to your spouse?

With Your Spouse

1. See if you can compliment each other all the way through the alphabet! For example, taking turns, start with the letter *A*, and say something to your spouse like, "You're the Apple of my eye," or, "You're Athletic," or, "I Admire you." Then go to the letter *B*, and try to make it all the way through the alphabet. If you make it through once, you may want to try for a second time with different words.

2. Share your answers to questions 1–4 that you did on your own. Be open, kind, and understanding toward each other.

3. Agree on any action steps you should take and how you should implement them.

4. Close by praying together, thanking God for your spouse.

Remember to take your calendar to the next session for Make a Date.

5

Freedom to
Fail

Separating self-worth from performance allows
people the freedom to take risks.

Big Dreams

Choose one of the following questions to answer and share with the
group:

- What is one of the riskiest things you have ever done
  or tried?
- If you knew you couldn't fail and money wasn't an issue,
  what is one dream you would pursue?
- What failure in your life can you look back at and appreciate in some way?

Project Report

Share one thing you learned from the HomeBuilders project from last session.

blueprints

Failure is inevitable in life. No one does it right every time. Our spouses can give us perspective and help us confront a challenge or deal with painful times—whether we have lost our keys or our jobs.

Failure can be divided into two categories:

- Failure that is sin (such as lying, lust, and greed)
- Failure that is not sin (such as honest mistakes, misunderstandings, and forgetting something)

While all sin is failure, not all failure is sin.

During this session we will look at the impact of sin and at some steps you can take to help each other deal with failure. The primary question is, how do you respond when your spouse faces failure?

The Impact of Failure

1. As a culture, we have developed a success syndrome that says only people who are healthy, wealthy, and powerful have worth and value. What do the following scriptures say about this philosophy?

- 1 Samuel 16:7

- Matthew 6:33

Six Steps to Giving Your Spouse the Freedom to Fail

During the remainder of this session, we will look at six steps that you and your spouse can take to give each other the freedom to risk failure and the strength to recover from it.

Step One: Offer forgiveness and restoration.
Read Luke 15:11–32.

2. From the story of the prodigal son, what can we tell about

- the son's feelings of worth in the midst of his failure?

- the father's response to his son's humility and desire for restoration?

3. What does this parable illustrate about God's love and acceptance of you? What is the lesson here for you on responding when your spouse fails?

Step Two: Assure your spouse of your commitment, loyalty, and love regardless of performance.
Read 1 John 4:18.

4. How can the assurance of your spouse's love help you when you are going through a difficult time?

Step Three: Remind your spouse, "Your worth is not in what you do but in who you are."
Read Ephesians 1:13–14.

5. How can a person fail without being a failure? When your spouse fails, how can you send the clear message that he or she is not a failure?

Step Four: Comfort your spouse with the truth that God is in control.
Read Romans 8:28.

6. Share an incident in which God brought good out of one of your failures.

Step Five: Join with your spouse in giving thanks in all things.
Read 1 Thessalonians 5:18.

7. Why should we thank God even amid our failures?

Step Six: Encourage your spouse not to lose heart when failure occurs.

Read 2 Corinthians 4:16–18.

8. How can your spouse best encourage you during difficult times?

homebuilders principle: When you give your spouse the freedom to fail, failure can become a tutor and not a judge.

9. Look at the following scenarios, and discuss how the previous steps could be applied to these situations.

- Howard is habitually late. He's late to work, late in coming home, and late to church. What can his wife do to help him?

- Sue has a great idea for a business but lacks the confidence to move beyond the idea. What can her husband do to help her?

- Tom just lost his job due to downsizing. What can his wife do to help him?

- Mary freezes up when making decisions. She tries to avoid situations in which she has to decide quickly. What can her husband do to help her?

make a date

Set a time for you and your spouse to complete the HomeBuilders project together before the next group meeting. You will be asked at the next session to share an insight or experience from the project.

date _____ time _____

location _____

homebuilders project

On Your Own

Answer the following questions:

1. Look through the Blueprints section, and name one important idea or technique you learned.

2. What is a failure you have experienced in your marriage?

3. What effect has this had on your marriage?

4. Which of the six steps studied in this session does your spouse do best? Give an example.

5. Which of the steps do you need to use more to help your spouse?

6. In your life right now, how willing are you to take risks, despite the fear of failure? Evaluate your current risk factor on a scale of 1 (no willingness to risk) to 10 (freely willing to risk). What ranking did you give yourself and why?

7. Where do you most fear failure? Circle the top two.

  at work
  as a husband or wife
  as a parent
  in managing finances
  in managing the household
  in a new venture
  as a friend
  in your emotions
  as a Christian
  other: _____

8. Look over the six steps that follow. Place a star by the ones you need the most from your spouse.

    (1) Forgiveness and restoration

    (2) Assurance of commitment, loyalty, and love regardless of performance

    (3) Reminders that "My worth is not in what I do but in who I am"

    (4) Being comforted with the truth that God is in control

    (5) Joining your spouse in giving thanks in all things

(6) Encouragement from your spouse not to lose heart in the midst of failure

Under each starred step, write out a practical way your spouse could meet this need for you.

As a Couple

1. Share the following with each other:

   - What do you most remember wanting to do or be when you grew up?

   - As you grew up, what things either encouraged or discouraged you from achieving your dreams?

   - What is one dream you have now—no matter how far-fetched—that you would like to do or try someday?

2. Discuss the questions you answered on your own.

3. How can you make your marriage a safe place in which each of you can risk failure?

4. Together read 1 Peter 4:8. What perspective does this verse give you on your spouse's failures?

5. Pray together. Thank God for giving you the freedom to risk failure. Thank God that, by the power of the Holy Spirit, you and your spouse can express the same freedom to each other.

Remember to take your calendar to the next session for Make a Date.

6

Keeping Life
Manageable

Couples experience peace and balance in marriage as they help each other make wise choices.

A Piece of the Pie

In the diagram on the next page, graph your typical day like a pie chart. Assign times for the following activities:

> sleeping
>
> eating (including preparation time)
>
> driving
>
> working
>
> studying the Bible and praying
>
> doing chores (e.g., paying bills, laundry, errands)
>
> watching television

being on the Internet
spending time with your spouse
spending time with your children
exercising
other: _____

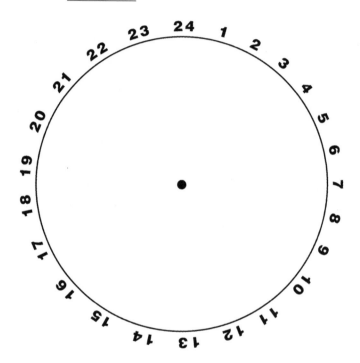

After charting your typical day, answer these questions:

- What priorities does your schedule reflect?

- Which areas in your life generally lose out to other things?

Project Report

Share one thing you learned from the HomeBuilders project from last session.

Stressed Out

1. From the following list, what are the top three factors that cause you stress?

   procrastination
   overcommitment
   job demands
   change
   conflict with a child or parent
   conflict with my spouse
   financial pressures
   unexpected problems
   recurring interpersonal friction

uncertain future
health problems
in-laws
friends
church involvement
my own unrealistic expectations
cultural pressures
other: _____

2. How does extra stress in your life affect the way you view
   yourself? The way you view your spouse?

Be Wise

Your real priorities are revealed by the choices you make each day.
These choices are a reflection of your true values. Your calendar and
checkbook are two significant indicators of your priorities—and
your values.

One of the shortcomings of many couples today is that they do
not take the necessary time to discuss values as a couple. A couple's
priorities will reflect their real values.

3. Read Ephesians 5:15–17. What does this passage teach us about determining our priorities? How can these principles help you handle stress?

4. Read James 1:5–6. How can you take greater advantage of what God offers here?

5. Look at the pie chart you made during Warm-Up. How could you change your schedule to reduce stress in your life?

Live by the Spirit

Ephesians 5:18 exhorts us to "be filled" with the Holy Spirit, which means to allow the Spirit to direct and empower us.

6. Read John 14:26–27 and Galatians 5:22–23. What do these verses tell you about the difference the Holy Spirit can make in your life?

7. How would the work of the Holy Spirit in a person's life affect his or her confidence? Explain.

8. Read Philippians 4:6–7. What role can prayer play in relieving stress?

homebuilders principle: Through prayer you and your spouse can ask God for wisdom to handle the pressures of life. His Holy Spirit can bring discernment, direction, peace, and order to your lives and marriage.

Submit to One Another

9. Read Ephesians 5:21. How can submitting to each other help prevent you and your spouse from becoming overcommitted or overly stressed?

homebuilders principle: God has given your spouse to you to help you find peace, direction, and balance in life.

make a date

Set a time for you and your spouse to complete the HomeBuilders project together before the next group meeting. You will be asked at the next session to share an insight or experience from the project.

date _____ time _____

location _____

homebuilders project

On Your Own

Answer the following questions:

1. As you look back at the information in this session, what is the best thing you can do to help make your spouse's life more manageable?

2. What is causing stress in your life right now? List three to five causes, if possible.

3. What do you think is causing the most stress in your spouse's life right now?

4. What five values are most important in your life?

5. Look over your calendar and checkbook for the last month. What priorities and values do they indicate?

6. Look back at the pie chart you did in the Warm-Up. What would you like to change in your schedule, and what steps do you need to take to begin this process?

7. How can your spouse help you live in a way that better reflects the values you desire for your life?

As a Couple

Answer the remaining questions.

1. We all need a day of refreshing now and then to help us cope with the stress of everyday living. Take a few minutes to plan the perfect day for your spouse. Write down what this day would look like and then share your plans with each other.

2. Compare your responses to the questions you answered on your own.

3. Together list the items that are causing stress in your lives (refer to questions 2 and 3 that you answered on your own), categorizing them in the chart below.

Things We Can Control	Things We Cannot Control

4. What decisions need to be made about the items under "Things We Can Control" to help your lives more clearly reflect your values?

5. Together decide on some specific ways each of you can help the other maintain a balanced lifestyle. List those ideas below.

6. Together read Matthew 11:28–30. How does that message relate to your lives and schedules?

7. Close your time in prayer, asking God for wisdom in helping each other to keep life manageable.

Remember to take your calendar to the next session for Make a Date.

Valuing Your
Spouse

Husbands and wives need to love, support, and encourage each other so they can become all that God intends them to be.

Looking Back

As you come to the end of this study, take some time to reflect as a group on what you have experienced. Pick one or more of the following questions to answer and share with the group.

- What has this group meant to you over the course of this study?
- What is the most valuable thing you have learned or discovered?
- How have you or your marriage changed as a result of this course?
- What would you like to see happen next for this group?

Project Report

Share one thing you learned from the HomeBuilders project from last session.

For this session we recommend dividing into two groups—one for husbands and one for wives. The Blueprints questions for husbands start on this page and for wives on page 77.

For Husbands

Your Wife as a Partner

1. Read 1 Peter 3:7. What does this mean to you as a husband?

2. What comes to your mind when you think of a partner?

3. List three to five ways you need your wife. Share at least one with the group.

4. How can showing your need for your wife build her confidence?

Honoring Your Wife

5. First Peter 3:7 exhorts husbands to show honor to their wives. What are some ways you can communicate honor to your wife?

6. What are some ways husbands communicate disrespect and dishonor to their wives?

Encouraging Your Wife

7. Read Ephesians 5:22–29. What do you think it means for a husband to love his wife "as Christ loved the church"?

8. What are some ways a husband can help his wife grow and feel valued in the following areas?

- Spirituality

- Gifts, talents, and abilities

- Dreams and visions for the future

9. How does honoring and encouraging your wife give value to her? In what ways do you and your marriage benefit from this as well?

homebuilders principle: As a husband, you are called to love your wife and help her develop into the woman God made her to be.

For Wives

Respecting Your Husband

1. Read Ephesians 5:33. What does it mean to respect your husband?

2. Why do you think your husband needs your respect? How does it affect his confidence?

3. What are some ways you can demonstrate or communicate respect for your husband when

    • you feel he is being unreasonable?

    • you disagree with a decision he has made?

- you are frustrated by his lack of participation or interest in dealing with an issue?

- you feel he doesn't give you a chance to participate in family decisions?

Submitting to Your Husband

Perhaps no other word receives as negative a response from women as *submit*. However, we believe submission is a key element of what the Bible teaches about a wife's relationship with her husband.

4. Read Ephesians 5:22–27. What does this passage say about the responsibility of a wife and the responsibility of a husband?

5. Why do many women struggle with the concept of being submissive to their husbands?

6. How would being submissive to your husband help him become the man God intends for him to be?

Understanding Your Husband

7. One of the major sources of misunderstanding in a marriage is the difference between men and women. How is your husband different from you? For the following exercise, jot down some of the differences between you and your spouse. In what area are you the most different from your husband?

Area	Your Husband	You
ways of thinking		
approach to physical intimacy		
style of communicating		
approach to problems		
background		
methods of handling conflict		
approach to managing money		

8. What are some ways your marriage has benefited from the differences between you and your husband?

9. How do respecting and encouraging your husband bring value to him? In what ways do you and your marriage benefit from this as well?

homebuilders principle: A wife that loves and respects her husband will help him develop into the man God made him to be.

make a date

Set a time for you and your spouse to complete the last HomeBuilders project of the study.

date _____ time _____

location _____

homebuilders project

On Your Own

Answer the following questions:

1. List at least five positive character qualities that you respect and admire in your spouse.

2. What are some of your spouse's talents and strengths?

3. What are your spouse's dreams and goals? List as many as you can.

4. How can you encourage your spouse to achieve these goals?

5. Read Philippians 2:1–4. What does this passage say to you about how you are to value your spouse?

6. As you look back over the session, what is the most important point of action that you need to follow up on?

7. Organizations have mission statements to help guide their direction and evaluate their efforts. If you had a mission statement for yourself as a husband or wife, what would it say? Answer the following questions individually to help develop a personal mission statement for valuing your spouse.

   • Up to this point, what has been your major purpose and direction as a husband or wife?

   • As you look forward, what would you like as your major purpose and direction as a husband or wife?

   • What specific action can you take to carry out this mission?

8. Close by praying for your spouse and asking God to show you what it truly means to value him or her.

With Your Spouse

Discuss the following.

1. Congratulations—you've made it to the last project for this study! Reflect on how this study has affected your marriage by answering these questions:

   - How did you feel in the first meeting of this study? What expectations did you have for this course? How has your experience compared to your expectations?

   - What is something from this study that has helped your marriage?

   - What new thing did you learn about your spouse?

   - What has been the best part of this study for you?

2. Share with each other your responses to the questions you answered on your own.

3. What is a specific action you can take together to carry out the marriage mission statement you wrote?

4. Evaluate some things you might do together to continue building your marriage and building up each other. One thing you may want to consider is continuing to regularly set aside time as you have for these projects. You may also want to look at some ideas on page 87 in "Where Do You Go from Here?"

5. Close with a time of prayer, thanking God for each other and for your marriage—what He has done and will do!

For Extra Impact

RSVP: This exercise is something you and your spouse may want to do now, or you can save it for a later date.

Imagine you have just received the following letter from your spouse. How would you respond in writing? Use a separate sheet of paper, and write your response. (Be specific and express how you feel.)

My dearest husband/wife,

Thank you for choosing me to share your life. Thank you for your honesty and transparency. I know it can be painful at times.

Deep down inside I really know that you love me. But I need tangible reminders of your love. There is very little in this life that I value more than your love. I need it. I need you.

Could I ask a favor? I love to receive letters from you, but I don't ever want to ask for them . . . it takes all the fun out of receiving them if it's my idea. But would you write me a letter?

I need to know

- *how you appreciate me*
- *what I've done to show that I respect you*
- *how I've been an encouragement to you*

- *that you appreciate the little things I do for you*
- *that I have your unconditional acceptance just as I am (Is it there? I need to know.)*
- *how I am a partner with you*
- *what you like about me*
- *how I've changed for good or how you've seen me grow (I forget sometimes.)*
- *that you want to do what is best for me*
- *that you want to meet my friends*
- *that your love will persevere*

You can write it any way you'd like, but please tell me.

I love you,

Your husband/wife

P.S. I know I'm not perfect, but I'm glad we're in this thing together.

We hope that you have benefited from this study in the Home-Builders Couples Series® and that your marriage will continue to grow as you both submit your lives to Jesus Christ and build according to His blueprints. We also hope that you will reach out to strengthen other marriages in your local church and community. Your influence is needed.

A favorite World War II story illustrates this point clearly.

The year was 1940. The French army had just collapsed under Hitler's onslaught. The Dutch had folded, overwhelmed by the Nazi regime. The Belgians had surrendered. And the British army was trapped on the coast of France in the channel port of Dunkirk.

Two hundred twenty thousand of Britain's finest young men seemed doomed to die, turning the English Channel red with their blood. The Fuehrer's troops, only miles away in the hills of France, didn't realize how close to victory they actually were.

Any attempt at rescue seemed futile in the time remaining. A thin British navy—the professionals—told King George VI that they could save 17,000 troops at best. The House of Commons was warned to prepare for "hard and heavy tidings."

Politicians were paralyzed. The king was powerless. And the Allies could only watch as spectators from a distance. Then as the doom of the British army seemed imminent, a strange fleet appeared on the horizon of the English Channel—the wildest assortment of boats perhaps ever assembled in history. Trawlers, tugs, scows, fishing sloops, lifeboats, pleasure craft, smacks and coasters, sailboats, even the London fire-brigade flotilla. Ships manned by civilian volunteers—English fathers joining in the rescue of Britain's exhausted, bleeding sons.

William Manchester writes in his epic novel *The Last Lion* that what happened in 1940 at Dunkirk seems like a miracle. Not only were most of the British soldiers rescued but 118,000 other Allied troops as well.

Today the Christian home is much like those troops at Dunkirk—pressured, trapped, demoralized, and in need of help. The Christian community may be much like England—waiting for professionals to step in and save the family. But the problem is much too large for them to solve alone.

We need an all-out effort by men and women "sailing" to rescue the exhausted and wounded families. We need an outreach effort by common couples with faith in an uncommon God. For too long, married couples within the church have abdicated to those in full-time vocational ministry the privilege and responsibility of influencing others.

We challenge you to invest your lives in others, to join in the rescue. You and other couples around the world can team together to build thousands of marriages and families and, in doing so, continue to strengthen your own.

Be a HomeBuilder

Here are some practical ways you can make a difference in families today:

- Gather a group of four to seven couples and lead them through this HomeBuilders study. Consider challenging others in your church or community to form additional HomeBuilders groups.
- Commit to continue building marriages by doing another small-group study in the HomeBuilders Couples Series®.
- Consider using the *JESUS* film as an outreach. For more information contact FamilyLife at the number or website below.
- Host a dinner party. Invite families from your neighborhood to your home, and as a couple share your faith in Christ.
- If you have attended FamilyLife's Weekend to Remember® marriage getaway, consider offering to assist your pastor in counseling engaged couples, using the material you received.

For more information about these ministry opportunities, contact your local church or

FamilyLife
PO Box 7111
Little Rock, AR 72223
1-800-FL-TODAY
FamilyLife.com

Every couple has to deal with problems in marriage—communication problems, money problems, difficulties with sexual intimacy, and more. Learning how to handle these issues is important to cultivating a strong and loving relationship.

The Big Problem

One basic problem is at the heart of every other problem in marriage, and it's too big for any person to deal with on his or her own. The problem is separation from God. If you want to experience life and marriage the way they were designed to be, you need a vital relationship with the God who created you.

But sin separates us from God. Some try to deal with sin by working hard to become better people. They may read books on how to control anger, or they may resolve to stop cheating on their taxes, but in their hearts they know—we all know—that the sin problem runs much deeper than bad habits and will take more than our best behavior to overcome it. In reality, we have rebelled against God. We have ignored Him and have decided to run our lives in a way that makes sense to us, thinking that our ideas and plans are better than His.

> For all have sinned and fall short of the glory of God.
> (Romans 3:23)

What does it mean to "fall short of the glory of God"? It means that none of us has trusted and treasured God the way we should. We have sought to satisfy ourselves with other things and have treated them as more valuable than God. We have gone our own way. According to the Bible, we have to pay a penalty for our sin. We cannot simply do things the way we choose and hope it will be okay with God. Following our own plans leads to our destruction.

> There is a way that seems right to a man, but its end
> is the way to death. (Proverbs 14:12)

> For the wages of sin is death. (Romans 6:23)

The penalty for sin is that we are separated from God's love. God is holy, and we are sinful. No matter how hard we try, we cannot come up with some plan, like living a good life or even trying to do what the Bible says, and hope that we can avoid the penalty.

God's Solution to Sin

Thankfully, God has a way to solve our dilemma. He became a man through the person of Jesus Christ. Jesus lived a holy life in perfect obedience to God's plan. He also willingly died on a cross to pay our penalty for sin. Then He proved that He is more powerful than sin or death by rising from the dead. He alone has the power to overrule the penalty for our sin.

> Jesus said to him, "I am the way, and the truth, and the
> life. No one comes to the Father except through me."
> (John 14:6)

But God shows his love for us in that while we were still sinners, Christ died for us. (Romans 5:8)

For the wages of sin is death, but the free gift of God is eternal life in Christ Jesus our Lord. (Romans 6:23)

The death and resurrection of Jesus have fixed our sin problem. He has bridged the gap between God and us. He is calling us to come to Him and to give up our flawed plans for running our lives. He wants us to trust God and His plan.

Accepting God's Solution

If you recognize that you are separated from God, He is calling you to confess your sins. All of us have made messes of our lives because we have stubbornly preferred our ideas and plans to His. As a result, we deserve to be cut off from God's love and His care for us. But God has promised that if we will acknowledge that we have rebelled against His plan, He will forgive us and will fix our sin problem.

But to all who did receive him, who believed in his name, he gave the right to become children of God. (John 1:12)

For by grace you have been saved through faith. And this is not your own doing; it is the gift of God, not a result of works, so that no one may boast. (Ephesians 2:8–9)

When the Bible talks about receiving Christ, it means we acknowledge that we are sinners and that we can't fix the problem ourselves. It means we turn away from our sin. And it means we trust Christ to forgive our sins and to make us the kind of people He wants us to be. It's not enough to intellectually believe that Christ is the Son of God. We must trust in Him and His plan for our lives by faith, as an act of the will.

Are things right between you and God, with Him and His plan at the center of your life? Or is life spinning out of control as you seek to make your own way?

If you have been trying to make your own way, you can decide today to change. You can turn to Christ and allow Him to transform your life. All you need to do is talk to Him and tell Him what is stirring in your mind and in your heart. If you've never done this, consider taking the steps listed here:

- Do you agree that you need God? Tell God.
- Have you made a mess of your life by following your own plan? Tell God.
- Do you want God to forgive you? Tell God.
- Do you believe that Jesus' death on the cross and His resurrection from the dead gave Him the power to fix your sin problem and to grant you the free gift of eternal life? Tell God.
- Are you ready to acknowledge that God's plan for your life is better than any plan you could come up with? Tell God.
- Do you agree that God has the right to be the Lord and Master of your life? Tell God.

Seek the LORD while he may be found; call upon him while he is near. (Isaiah 55:6)

Here is a suggested prayer:

Lord Jesus, I need You. Thank You for dying on the cross for my sins. I receive You as my Savior and Lord. Thank You for forgiving my sins and giving me eternal life. Make me the kind of person You want me to be.

The Christian Life

For the person who is a follower of Christ—a Christian—the penalty for sin is paid in full. But the effect of sin continues throughout our lives.

> If we say we have no sin, we deceive ourselves, and the truth is not in us. (1 John 1:8)

> For I do not do the good I want, but the evil I do not want is what I keep on doing. (Romans 7:19)

The effects of sin carry over into our marriages as well. Even Christians struggle to maintain solid, God-honoring marriages. Most couples eventually realize they can't do it on their own. But with God's help, they can succeed.

To learn more, read the extended version of this article at FamilyLife.com/Resources.

leader's notes

What is the leader's job?

Your role is more of a facilitator than a teacher. A teacher usually does most of the talking and instructing whereas a facilitator encourages people to think and to discover what the Scripture says. You should help group members feel comfortable and keep things moving forward.

Is there a structure to the sessions?

Yes, each session is composed of the following categories:

Warm-Up (5–10 minutes): The purpose of Warm-Up is to help people unwind from a busy day and get to know one another better. Typically the Warm-Up starts with an exercise that is fun but also introduces the topic of the session.

Blueprints (45–50 minutes): This is the heart of the study when people answer questions related to the topic of study and look to God's Word for understanding. Some of the questions are to be discussed between spouses and others with the whole group.

HomeBuilders Project (60 minutes): This project is the unique application that couples will work on between the group meetings. Each HomeBuilders project contains two sections: (1) On your own—questions for husbands and wives to answer individually and (2) With your spouse—an opportunity for couples to share their answers with each other and to make application in their lives.

In addition to these regular features, occasional activities are labeled "For Extra Impact." These activities provide a more active or visual way to make a particular point.

What is the best setting and time schedule for this study?

This study is designed as a small-group, home Bible study. However, it can be adapted for more structured settings like a Sunday school class. Here are some suggestions for using this study in various settings:

In a small group

To create a friendly and comfortable atmosphere, we recommend you do this study in a home setting. In many cases the couple that leads the study also serves as host, but sometimes involving another couple as host is a good idea. Choose the option you believe will work best for your group, taking into account factors such as the number of couples participating and the location.

Each session is designed as a sixty-minute study, but we recommend a ninety-minute block of time to allow for more relaxed conversation and refreshments. Be sure to keep in mind one of the cardinal rules of a small group: good groups start *and* end on time. People's time is valuable, and your group will appreciate your respecting this.

In a Sunday school class

If you want to use the study in a class setting, you need to adapt it in two important ways: (1) You should focus on the content of the Blueprints section of each session. That is the heart of the session.

(2) Many Sunday school classes use a teacher format instead of a small-group format. If this study is used in a class setting, the class should adapt to a small-group dynamic. This will involve an interactive, discussion-based format and may also require a class to break into multiple smaller groups.

What is the best size group?

We recommend from four to seven couples (including you and your spouse). If more people are interested than you can accommodate, consider asking someone to lead a second group. If you have a large group, you may find it beneficial to break into smaller subgroups on occasion. This helps you cover the material in a timely fashion and allows for optimum interaction and participation within the group.

What about refreshments?

Many groups choose to serve refreshments, which helps create an environment of fellowship. If you plan to include refreshments, here are a couple of suggestions: (1) For the first session (or two) you should provide the refreshments. Then involve the group by having people sign up to bring them on later dates. (2) Consider starting your group with a short time of informal fellowship and refreshments (15–20 minutes). Then move into the study. If couples are late, they miss only the food and don't disrupt the study. You may also want to have refreshments available again at the end of your meeting to encourage fellowship. But remember to respect the group members' time by ending the session on schedule and allowing anyone who needs to leave to do so gracefully.

What about child care?

Groups handle this differently, depending on their needs. Here are a couple of options you may want to consider:

- Have people be responsible for making their own arrangements.
- As a group, hire someone to provide child care, and have all the children watched in one location.

What about prayer?

An important part of a small group is prayer. However, as the leader, you need to be sensitive to people's comfort level with praying in front of others. Never call on people to pray aloud unless you know they are comfortable doing this. You can take creative approaches, such as modeling prayer, calling for volunteers, and letting people state their prayers in the form of finishing a sentence. A helpful tool in a group is a prayer list. You should lead the prayer time, but allow another couple to create, update, and distribute prayer lists as their ministry to the group.

Find additional help and suggestions for leading your HomeBuilders group at FamilyLife.com/Resources.

The sessions in this study can be easily led without a lot of preparation time. However, accompanying Leader's Notes have been provided to assist you when needed. The categories within the Leader's Notes are as follows:

Objectives

The Objectives focus on the issues that will be presented in each session.

Notes and Tips

This section provides general ideas, helps, and suggestions about the session. You may want to create a checklist of things to include in each session.

Blueprints Commentary

This section contains notes that relate to the Blueprints questions. Not all Blueprints questions will have accompanying commentary notes. The number of the commentary note corresponds to the number of the question it relates to. (For example, the Leader's Notes, session 1, number 5 in the Blueprints Commentary section relates back to session 1, Blueprints, question 5.)

session one

giving strength to the one you love

Objectives

Marriage provides one of life's best relationships for building a person's confidence and courage.

In this session couples will

- share experiences from early in their marriages,
- discover the importance of building up each other,
- understand how an unrealistic image of the ideal husband or wife may have distorted their self-perception, and
- begin building up their spouses.

Notes and Tips

1. If you have not already done so, you will want to read the information "About Leading a HomeBuilders Group" and "About the Leader's Notes," starting on page 99.

2. As part of the first session, you may want to review with the group some ground rules (see page vii in "Welcome to HomeBuilders").

3. At this first meeting collect the names, phone numbers, and e-mail addresses of the group members. You may want to make a list to copy and distribute to the entire group.

4. Because this is the first session, make a special point to tell the group about the importance of the HomeBuilders project. Encourage each couple to make a date for a time to complete the project before the next meeting. Mention that you will ask about this during Warm-Up at the next session.

5. If this group has not been together before, you may want to have couples introduce themselves as part of the Warm-Up time. One way to do this is to have couples briefly share how and when they met. If you do this, be aware that you will probably spend more time than normal in Warm-Up and may not get to all the discussion questions. You might find it helpful to mark the Blueprints questions that you want to be sure to cover.

6. You may want to offer the closing prayer yourself instead of asking others to pray aloud. Many people are uncomfortable praying in front of others, and unless you already know your group well, it may be wise to venture slowly into various methods of prayer. Regardless of how you decide to close, you should serve as a model.

7. If there is room for more people, you may want to remind the group that they can still invite another couple to join them since this study is just under way.

8. Session 1 sets the tone for the series and builds a couple's appreciation for building up each other's confidence and

self-esteem. To accomplish this, the session must be fun and memorable. Do not allow the group to bog down in any areas of discussion or linger on anything negative.

Blueprints Commentary

Here is some additional information about one of the Blueprints questions. (Note: the number below corresponds to the Blueprints question it relates to.) Throughout the series, if you share any of the Blueprints points, do so in a manner that does not stifle discussion by making you the authority with the real answers. Begin your comments by saying things like, "One thing I notice in this passage is . . ." or, "I think another reason for this is . . ."

7. You may want to point out that God's truth contrasts with the phantom truth in that it expresses what is real.

session two

unconditional acceptance

Objectives

Spouses can give each other the liberating power of unconditional love.

In this session couples will

- discover their individual need of acceptance and the importance of acceptance in building their spouse's confidence,
- evaluate their commitment to accept their spouses,
- explore two biblical components of acceptance, and
- practice expressing acceptance with their spouses.

Notes and Tips

1. Since this is the second session, your group members have probably warmed up a bit to one another but may not yet feel free to be completely open and honest about their relationships. Don't force the issue. Continue to encourage couples to attend and to complete their projects.

2. If someone in this session has joined the group for the first time, give a brief summary of the main points of session 1. Also be sure to introduce those who do not know each other. And consider giving new couples the chance to tell when and where they met.

3. If refreshments are planned for this session, make sure arrangements for them have been made.

4. If your group has decided to use a prayer list, make sure this is covered.

5. If you told the group during the first session that you'd be asking them to share something they learned from the first HomeBuilders project, be sure to ask them. This is an important way for you to establish an environment of accountability.

6. The benefits of prayer is probably the most important topic of this session. If your group members understand that prayer doesn't have to be lifeless—that they can grow spiritually and experience God and His peace—they'll be motivated to pray more.

7. You may want to ask for a volunteer to close the session in prayer. Check ahead of time with people you think might be comfortable praying aloud.

8. Call attention to the "For Extra Impact" exercise that appears at the end of the HomeBuilders project for this session. Encourage the couples to do this exercise, even at a later date if necessary.

Blueprints Commentary

1. Adam and Eve hid from God. They feared rejection from Him.

2. People want others to like them, so they often don't have enough confidence to stand up to rejection. For many this stems from a childhood in which they never felt accepted.

4. God loved us when we were still sinful. God raised us up with Christ and seated us with Him in the heavenly places. God wanted to show us the mercy and riches of His grace.

5. Adam knew God and trusted His provision.

session three

putting the past in perspective

Objectives

Understanding how the past has affected a spouse's self-perception can build hope and perspective.

In this session couples will,

- discover the power of forgiveness as found in the gospel of Jesus Christ,
- evaluate their own attitudes about failures in the past as compared with God's Word,
- explore the proper way of looking back and living today, and
- practice God's forgiveness in their own lives and toward their spouses.

Notes and Tips

1. This session focuses on creating hope for being liberated from the past. Perhaps no other session in this study is more delicate and potentially threatening than this one. Many couples don't realize how much the events of their pasts can influence their marriage. Recognize the potential for both good and harm in this session, and approach it carefully and with prayer.

Regardless of what happened in a person's past, it is important to deal with this subject in both a frank and sensitive manner during the Bible study. While people need to confront their pasts honestly, no one should share anything that would be embarrassing to his or her spouse or that might damage or harm anyone else.

A person can move forward from his past, but first he must deal with guilt and condemnation. Forgiveness must be experienced vertically with God through Jesus Christ, then horizontally with people.

2. Sometime during this session a person may ask, "How much of my past should I share with my spouse?" Ideally, oneness between two people means no secrets. However, we do not live in an ideal world, and information from the past can be very difficult for someone to handle. Before sharing information that could damage a relationship, one should seek wise counsel to help evaluate whether the information should be discussed with a counselor first.

3. Remember the importance of starting and ending on time.

4. As an example to the group, you and your spouse should complete the HomeBuilders project for each session.

5. You may find it helpful to make some notes right after the meeting to evaluate how things went. Ask yourself questions such as, Did everyone participate? Is there anyone I need to follow up with before the next session?

Blueprints Commentary

4. We must trust what God is doing now and not dwell on past defeats.

5. If there are people in your group who are not familiar with the life of the apostle Paul, you may want to talk briefly about his life. See Acts 22, Acts 26, and 2 Corinthians 11:16–33 for details.

7. Obviously, we should forgive. But forgiving someone who has caused deep hurt is very difficult, if not impossible, for someone who has never experienced God's forgiveness.

Ephesians 4:32 summarizes how best to deal with offenses in our own past and to help our spouse do the same. This verse calls us to deal with the past of others as God has dealt with our past and to initiate kind, loving actions in the present. You may want to pose this question: "Since God has been kind and loving toward you and has given up His right to punish you, how should you and your spouse respond to each other's past mistakes?"

You may also want to share the following definition of forgiveness: "To forgive means to put away the right to punish another, to respond to past failures without resentment or accusation."

session four

planting positive words

Objectives

The words people speak have the potential to build up or tear down
their spouses.

In this session couples will

- examine biblical and personal insights into the power
  of words,
- evaluate their expressions of praise to their spouses, and
- identify praiseworthy qualities possessed by their
  spouses.

Notes and Tips

1. Congratulations. With the completion of this session, you
   will be more than halfway through this study. It's time for
   a checkup: How are you feeling? How is the group going?
   What has worked well so far? What things would you
   consider changing as you head into the second half?

2. This can be the most enjoyable session of the study as its
   focus is highly positive. Everyone enjoys being compli-
   mented. Beyond making people feel good, positive words can

have a lasting impact on an individual and on a marriage. The converse is also true; negative words can have a profoundly harmful impact.

3. For the Warm-Up in this session, group members will guess the identity of one another based on a list of descriptive words that they wrote about themselves and that you read to the group. To make this more interesting, suggest to the group that they use descriptions that are not immediately obvious. For example, if one person in the group has red hair, that person should not use *redheaded* as a description. It is better to list traits, talents, or tendencies (shyness, tennis player, procrastinator). You will need to have paper or index cards for this exercise.

4. By this time group members should be getting comfortable with each other. For prayer at the end of this session, you may want to give anyone who wishes an opportunity to pray by asking the group to finish a sentence that starts something like this: *"Lord, I want to thank You for* _____." Be sensitive to those who are not comfortable doing this.

5. This week you and your spouse may want to write notes of thanks and encouragement to the couples in your group. Thank them for their commitment and contribution, and let them know you are praying for them. (Make a point to pray for them as you write their note.)

Blueprints Commentary

1. For many people the reality is that words hurt much more than sticks and stones would.

6. People can find it hard to give praise for several reasons: They have rarely received it, so they don't know how. They may feel they should praise others sparingly so that their position of authority and power is strengthened. Also, some find it easier to poke fun or playfully disagree than to express affirmation and support. Sometimes this person has good intentions but simply does not feel comfortable directly expressing a positive emotion.

   People can find it hard to receive praise if they sense it isn't honest appreciation. When praise comes from someone whose attitudes and actions are not in tune, people feel they are being flattered or manipulated.

session five

freedom to fail

Objectives

Separating self-worth from performance allows people the freedom
to take risks.

In this session couples will

- describe past situations in which they failed,
- examine the negative consequences of fear of failure, and
- explore the biblical perspective on true success.

Notes and Tips

1. In this session you deal with the subject of failure. It might
   be wise to remind the group not to share anything that would
   embarrass their spouses.

2. If you believe there are people in your group who are strug-
   gling with overcoming past failure due to sin, you may want
   to encourage them to read the article "Our Problems, God's
   Answers" that appears in their books.

3. As the leader of a small group, one of the best things you can
   do for your group is to pray specifically for each member. Why
   not take some time to pray as you prepare for this session?

Blueprints Commentary

1. You might want to make these points from these scriptures:

   - 1 Samuel 16:7—God looks at the heart, not the outer appearance.
   - Matthew 6:33—God's kingdom is the foundation upon which any good thing in life must be built.

   If we are going to learn to handle failure and the risk of failure, we must start with the understanding that true success in life is very different from the surface trappings of success that tend to consume so much of our physical and emotional energy.

2. In the prodigal son story we find

   - the prodigal felt unworthy to be a son and
   - the father was full of compassion and forgiveness.

3. God is always ready to forgive and restore; we should be willing to do the same.

4. Such assurance gives you greater freedom to risk failure in those hard times.

session six

keeping life manageable

Objectives

Couples experience peace and balance in marriage as they help each other make wise choices.

In this session couples will

- disclose factors that contribute to stress,
- examine three biblical principles for determining priorities,
- consider how being filled with the Holy Spirit enables a person to handle the stresses of life successfully, and
- pray as a couple about dealing with specific stresses.

Notes and Tips

1. In Warm-Up the group is charting a typical day. If people have trouble figuring out what their typical day looks like, you could suggest they chart what yesterday was like for them.

2. Looking ahead: For Blueprints in session 7, husbands and wives will be in two different groups. For this part of the study, you will need to have a person lead the group you're not in. Be sure to make arrangements for this ahead of time. Your spouse may be a good choice for this.

3. Looking ahead (part two): For the next session—the last session of this study—you may want to have a person or a couple share what this study or group has meant to them.

Blueprints Commentary

3. We should be wise in the way we live, making the most of our time. We should turn away from what is foolish and toward what God would have us do.

9. One way would be to agree to check with your spouse before accepting a commitment. This provides a time and thought buffer and invites the other person's feedback in advance of a decision.

session seven

valuing your spouse

Objectives

Husbands and wives need to love, support, and encourage each other so they can become all that God intends them to be.

In this session couples will

- affirm their need for their spouses;
- discuss the importance of understanding, respecting, and encouraging their spouses; and
- work together to develop a mission statement for their marriages.

Notes and Tips

1. While this HomeBuilders Couples Series® has great value, people are likely to gradually return to previous patterns of living unless they commit to a plan for carrying on the progress made. During this final session, encourage couples to take specific steps beyond this series to keep their marriages growing. For example, you may want to challenge couples who have developed the habit of a date night during the course of this study to continue this practice. Also, you may want the group to consider doing another study from this series.

2. Session 7 is unique because husbands and wives will meet in separate groups for the Blueprints section. The purpose is to facilitate a more open discussion of issues related to how they value their spouses.

3. Arrange ahead of time for two comfortable rooms where the groups can meet and not disturb each other.

4. Be sure to allow enough time for the last question in Blueprints (both for husbands and wives).

5. There is a "For Extra Impact" exercise at the end of the HomeBuilders project. You should bring this to the group's attention as the couples may want to set aside extra time to complete it.

6. As a part of this last session, you may want to devote some time to planning one more meeting—a party to celebrate the completion of this study!

Blueprints Commentary

For Husbands

4. A person's sense of value is strongly influenced by knowing that he or she matters to someone.

For Wives

5. One factor that has contributed to tensions between men and women is the cultural pressure that pushes wives to be independent of their husbands. That message from the culture conflicts with this passage from Ephesians 5. Husbands and wives need each other.

Looking for more ways to help people build their marriages and families?

Thank you for your efforts to help people develop their marriages and families using biblical principles. We recognize the influence that one person—or couple—can have on another, and we'd like to help you multiply your ministry.

FamilyLife® is pleased to offer a wide range of resources in various formats. Visit us online at FamilyLife.com, where you will find information about our:

- getaways and events, featuring Weekend to Remember® and the Art of Marriage®, offered in cities throughout the United States;
- multimedia resources for small groups, churches, and community networking;
- interactive products for parents, couples, small-group leaders, and one-to-one mentors; and
- assortment of blogs, forums, and other online connections.

FamilyLife® is a nonprofit, Christian organization focused on the mission of helping every home become a godly home. Believing that family is the foundation of society, FamilyLife works in more than a hundred countries around the world to build healthier marriages and families through marriage getaways and events, small-group curriculum, *FamilyLife Today*® radio broadcasts, Hope for Orphans® orphan care ministry, the Internet, and a wide range of marriage and family resources.

 Dennis and Barbara Rainey are cofounders of FamilyLife. Authors of over twenty-five books and hundreds of articles, they are also popular conference speakers and radio hosts. With six grown children and numerous grandchildren, the Raineys love to encourage couples in building godly marriages and families.